WORD PROBLEMS: MASS AND VOLUME

1 LITER
1000ml
950 — 900
850 — 800
750 — 700
650 — 600
550 — 500
450 — 400
350 — 300

Helen Mason

Crabtree Publishing Company

www.crabtreebooks.com

Writing team: Helen Mason, Reagan Miller, Crystal Sikkens
Publishing plan research and development:
 Sean Charlebois, Reagan Miller
 Crabtree Publishing Company
Editors: Ruth Frederick, Leslie Jenkins, Phyllis Jelinek, Dana Freeman
Proofreader: Lisa Slone
Editorial director: Kathy Middleton
Production coordinator: Shivi Sharma
Creative director: Amir Abbasi
Design: Samara Parent
Cover design: Margaret Amy Salter
Photo research: Nivisha Sinha, Crystal Sikkens
Production coordinator and prepress technician: Samara Parent
Print coordinators: Katherine Berti, Margaret Amy Salter

Photographs:
Cover: Shutterstock; Page 1: Tyler Olson/Shutterstock (girl), You Touch Pix of EuToch/Shutterstock (measuring cup); Page 4: Monkey Business Images/Shutterstock; Page 5: Lars Hallstrom/Shutterstock (dropper), STEVEN CHIANG/Shutterstock (glass), ericlefrancais/Shutterstock (cream), trubach/Shutterstock (milk); Page 6: studioVin/Shutterstock (left), Purestock/Thinkstock (right); Page 7: Peter Witkop/Shutterstock (top), PRILL/Shutterstock (bottom); Page 8: Suzanne Tucker/Shutterstock; Page 10: Dmitriy Kalinin/Shutterstock; Page 11: Steve Collender/Shutterstock; Page 12: artzenter/Shutterstock; Page 14: imagedb.com/Shutterstock (spoon), mexrix/Shutterstock (fork); Page 15: Kitch Bain/Shutterstock (book), Robert Spriggs/Shutterstock (butter), Robyn Mackenzie/iStockphoto (golf ball), Africa Studio/Shutterstock (shoelace), zentilia/Shutterstock (car); Page 16: iStockphoto/Thinkstock; Page 18: Molly70photo/Shutterstock; Page 19: blackman/Shutterstock; Page 20: SeDmi/Shutterstock; Page 21: Coprid/Shutterstock (stones), magicoven/Shutterstock (pot): Page 22: Lars Hallstrom/Shutterstock (dropper), STEVEN CHIANG/Shutterstock (glass), ericlefrancais/Shutterstock (cream), trubach/Shutterstock (milk); Page 23: Kitch Bain/Shutterstock (book), Robert Spriggs/Shutterstock (butter), Robyn Mackenzie/iStockphoto (golf ball)

Artwork Created by Planman technologies: Pages 14, 15 (paperclip)

Library and Archives Canada Cataloguing in Publication

Mason, Helen, 1950-
 Word problems : mass and volume / Helen Mason.

(My path to math)
Includes index.
Issued in print and electronic formats.
ISBN 978-0-7787-1081-3 (bound).--ISBN 978-0-7787-1097-4 (pbk.)
ISBN 978-1-4271-9275-2 (pdf).--ISBN 978-1-4271-9199-1 (html)

 1. Word problems (Mathematics)--Juvenile literature. 2. Mass (Physics)--Measurement--Juvenile literature. 3. Volume (Cubic content)--Juvenile literature. I. Title. II. Series: My path to math

QA63.M37 2013   j510   C2013-902668-1
                                     C2013-902669-X

Library of Congress Cataloging-in-Publication Data

CIP available at Library of Congress

Crabtree Publishing Company
www.crabtreebooks.com   1-800-387-7650

Printed in the USA/052013/JA20130412

Published in Canada
Crabtree Publishing
616 Welland Ave.
St. Catharines, ON
L2M 5V6

Published in the United States
Crabtree Publishing
PMB 59051
350 Fifth Avenue, 59th Floor
New York, New York 10118

Published in the United Kingdom
Crabtree Publishing
Maritime House
Basin Road North, Hove
BN41 1WR

Published in Australia
Crabtree Publishing
3 Charles Street
Coburg North
VIC, 3058

Contents

What Is Volume?

Jada, Xavier, and their friends from school are busy getting ready for their school's fundraiser. The kids are going to sell milkshakes to raise money for new sports equipment. They want to make a big batch of milkshake and then separate it into smaller cups to sell. Jada tells her friends that she has the perfect container to hold their big batch of milkshake.

Xavier says that the container will be perfect for measuring the **volume** of the milkshake. Volume is the amount of space matter takes up. Everything around us is made up of **matter**, even you!

Volume can be measured in different units, such as ounces, pints, **quarts**, and **gallons**. It can also be measured in **milliliters** or **liters**. **Capacity** is the total amount of matter a container can hold.

One milliliter is about 20 drops of water.

A large glass holds 16 ounces or 1 pint of liquid.

A large carton of cream holds about one liter or one quart.

A jug of milk holds about one gallon.

Measuring Volume

To find the volume of a liquid, you must pour the liquid into a container that has liquid volume measurements labeled on it. The beaker and graduated cylinder are tools that can measure volume.

A graduated cylinder or beaker should be read at eye level.

beaker

When measuring liquid, always read the mark closest to the bottom of the **meniscus**. The meniscus is at the top of the liquid and slightly curves up the sides of the container.

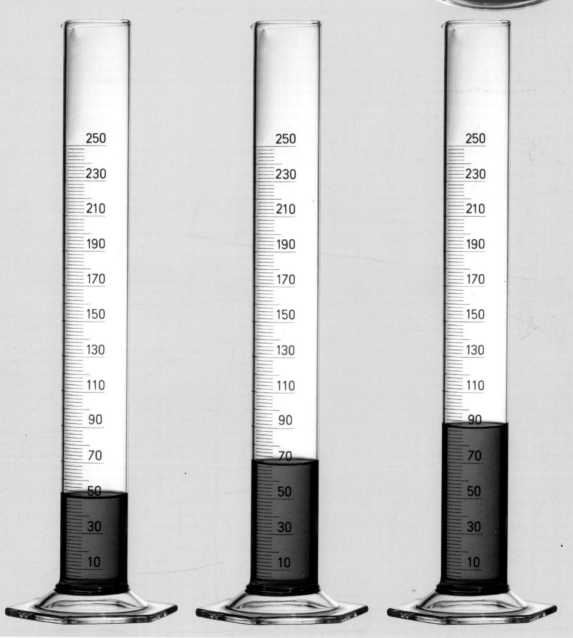

Activity Box

The graduated cylinders above are in milliliters. What volume is shown on each of the graduated cylinders?

Getting ready

Before they start making the milkshake, the kids must make sure they have all of the ingredients they need. Jada looks at the recipe and sees they need 750 ml of milk. She needs to go to the store to buy the milk. When she gets back, Xavier sees she has bought three cartons of milk. Each carton holds 250 ml. Did Jada buy enough milk for the milkshake?

The Milk Problem

Jada bought three cartons of milk at the store. Each carton holds 250 ml of milk. How much milk did she buy in all?

Xavier remembers some steps he learned at school to help him solve this problem.

Steps for Solving Word Problems

1. **Understand** — What does the problem ask you to do? What information do you have to solve it?
2. **Plan** — How can you solve the problem? What operations will you use? Set up the problem using numbers, pictures, or a model.
3. **Solve** — Do the math.
4. **Check** — Does the answer make sense?

Xavier's Thinking

I have to find out if the total amount of milk equals 750 ml. If I add together the amount of milk in all three containers, I should find out how much milk she bought in all.

250 ml + 250 ml + 250 ml = 750 ml

Xavier sees that she has bought enough milk for the milkshake.

Mix and Measure

The kids are working hard making their milkshake. They are trying to fill Jada's 20-liter container. Jada looks at the measurements on the container. They have made 12 liters of milkshake so far. An hour later, Jada sees that they have 19 liters of milkshake. How many liters of milkshake did they make in an hour?

The Milkshake Problem

The kids have made 12 liters of milkshake so far. An hour later, they have made 19 liters. How many liters of milkshake did they make in an hour?

Jada's Thinking

An hour ago there was 12 liters of milkshake. I know there is 19 liters in total now. I could subtract 19 liters from 12 liters to find out how much we made in an hour.

Jada draws a chart to help her solve the problem.

19 liters in total	
12 liters	?
amount to start with	amount added

Jada writes the problem as a number sentence and solves it:

19 liters – 12 liters = X

The kids made 7 liters of milkshake in an hour.

Activity Box

A soccer coach brought a water cooler to a game that had 25 L of water in it. After her soccer game the container had 18 L of water. How many liters of water did the players drink during the game? Explain how you know.

Solving Using Division

The 20-liter container is now filled with milkshake. Xavier tries to pick up the container, but it is too heavy! They will need to pour the milkshake into smaller containers so it is easier to carry. Xavier finds five containers to pour the milkshake in to. He wants to divide the milkshake into equal parts so each container has the same amount.

Dividing the Milkshake

Xavier needs to divide 20 liters of milkshake equally into 5 containers. How many liters should he pour into each container?

Xavier draws a picture to help him find out how many liters of milkshake to put in each container.

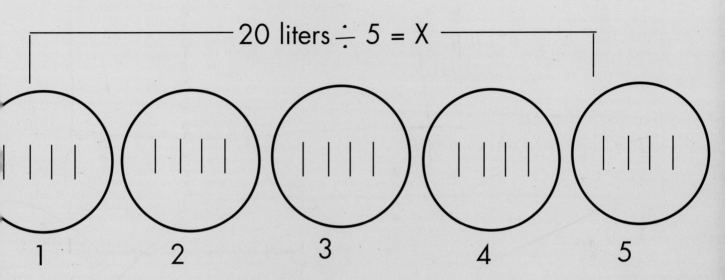

$$20 \text{ liters} \div 5 = X$$

1   2   3   4   5

He draws a circle for each of the five containers. He makes a tick in circle 1 that stands for 1 liter of milkshake. Then he makes a tick in circle 2. He continues making ticks in the 5 circles until he counts up to 20 ticks. Then he goes back and counts the number of ticks in each circle. How many liters should Xavier pour into each container?

Xavier's Thinking
Using tick marks will help me divide the liters of milkshake into the containers equally.

Activity Box

Create your own volume word problem. Make sure it can be solved by drawing a picture. Give your word problem to a friend. Check their work when they are done.

What Is Mass?

Mass is the amount of matter in something. Mass is usually measured by how much something weighs. One way to measure mass is to use a **balance**.

Arm

Balance

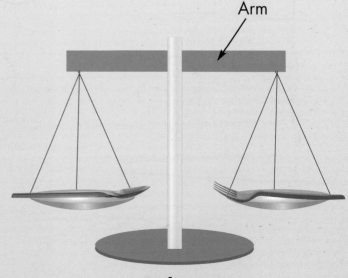

Balance

The left side of the balance is lower. The paper is heavier than the blocks. The right side is higher. The blocks are lighter than the paper.

The arm of the scale is even. One side is not heavier than the other side.

Mass can be measured in different units, such as grams, kilograms, ounces, and pounds.

A large paperclip weighs 1 gram.

A textbook weighs about 1 kilogram.

BUTTER

A golf ball weighs 1 ounce.

A brick of butter weighs about 1 pound.

Activity Box

What would you use to weigh each of these items?

☐ gram

☐ kilogram

☐ gram

☐ kilogram

Finding the Missing Mass

On the way to the fundraiser, the kids stop at the store to buy a box of straws and a box of cups. The store clerk weighs both boxes together and tells them that the total mass is 475 grams. Xavier looks at the box of straws and sees it is 125 grams. He asks Jada to find out what the mass is of the box of cups.

Find the Mass of the Cups

The total mass of the box of straws and box of cups is 475 grams. The mass of the box of straws is 125 grams. What is the mass of the box of cups?

Jada uses the information she knows to make a chart to help her solve the problem.

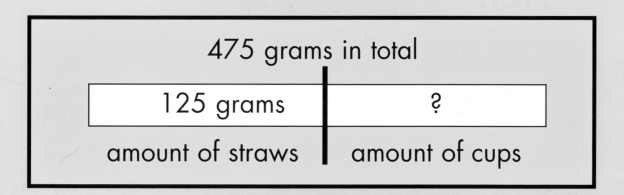

Jada writes the problem as a number sentence:
475 grams – 125 grams = X

She does the math to solve the problem.
Jada finds out the mass of the box of cups is 350 grams.

Activity Box

Use addition to check Jada's work above. What two amounts should you add together? Write a number sentence to show your work.
Hint: Your answer should be the total mass of the box of straws and the box of cups.

Solving Using Multiplication

The kids want to sell kiwi fruit along with their milkshakes at the fundraiser. They buy the kiwis while they are at the store. The store clerk weighs 1 kiwi. Its mass is 40 grams. The kids decide to buy 5 kiwis. Xavier wants to know what the total mass of the 5 kiwis is.

The Kiwi Problem

The mass of 1 kiwi is 40 grams. What is the total mass of 5 kiwis?

Xavier's Thinking

One kiwi has a mass of 40 grams. If I multiply that number by 5, I will get the total mass of the kiwis. I could draw a picture and count by 10 to help me multiply these numbers.

Xavier draws a picture using base ten blocks. He starts by drawing 5 kiwis. He knows the mass of each kiwi is 40 grams. Under each kiwi picture he draws 4 columns of base ten blocks. This will equal 40.

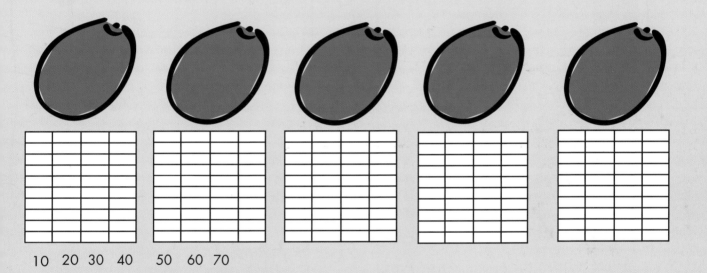

10 20 30 40   50 60 70

He counts the columns by 10s. Xavier writes his answer in a number sentence:

40 grams X 5 = 200 grams

The total mass of 5 kiwis is 200 grams.

More Mass Problems

The kids sell all their milkshakes and kiwis at the fundraiser. On their way home, they see Mr. Watts working in his garden. He wants to plant flowers in 4 pots. First he has to fill the pots with soil. He has a 32 kilogram bag of soil. He wants to divide the bag of soil between the pots so each pot has the same mass. He asks the kids to help him find out how many kilograms of soil he should put in each pot?

The Soil Problem

Mr. Watts has a 32 kilogram bag of soil. He wants to divide the bag equally into 4 pots. How many kilograms of soil should he put in each pot?

Jada uses Mr. Watts' 4 pots and some stones to help her solve the problem.

Jada lines up the 4 pots. She gathers 32 stones. Each stone stands for 1 kilogram. She puts one stone in each pot until she has used up all 32 stones. She then counts the stones in each pot and writes her answer as a number sentence:

32 kilograms ÷ 4 = 8 kilograms

Jada tells Mr. Watts he needs to put 8 kilograms of soil in each of his pots.

Activity Box

Use multiplication to check Jada's work above. What two numbers should you multiply together? Write a number sentence to show your work.

Glossary

balance A tool used for comparing the weight of two items; when the items are equal in weight, the arm of the balance will be level

capacity The total amount of matter a container can hold

gallon A unit for measuring large volumes; 1 gallon = 4 quarts or 3.785 liters

liter A unit for measuring volume, often used for milk and juice; a liter is slightly bigger than a quart

One milliliter is about 20 drops of water.

A large glass holds 16 ounces or 1 pint of liquid.

A carton of cream holds about one liter or one quart.

A jug of milk holds about one gallon.

mass The amount of matter in something; usually measured by how much something weighs

matter The material that everything in the universe is made of

meniscus The top of a liquid that curves up the sides of a container

milliliter A unit for measuring small volumes; 1000 milliliters = 1 liter

quart A unit for measuring volume, often used for milk and juice; a quart is slightly less than a liter

volume The amount of space that matter takes up; how much a container or space will hold

A large paperclip weighs 1 gram.

A textbook weighs about 1 kilogram.

A golf ball weighs 1 ounce.

A brick of butter weighs about 1 pound.

Index

Learn More

Crickweb www.crickweb.co.uk/ks2numeracy-shape-and-weight.html#fruitbalance3

IXL http://ca.ixl.com/math/grade-2/which-metric-unit-of-volume-is-appropriate

http://ca.ixl.com/math/grade-2/choose-the-appropriate-measuring-tool

http://ca.ixl.com/math/grade-2/compare-size-mass-and-capacity

http://ca.ixl.com/math/grade-3/which-metric-unit-of-volume-is-appropriate

http://ca.ixl.com/math/grade-3/which-metric-unit-of-mass-is-appropriate

Harcourt School Publishing www.harcourtschool.com/activity/ounces_pounds/

www.harcourtschool.com/activity/pounds/

Math Playground www.mathplayground.com/balance_scales.html